Faith in Motion: The Workbook

Faith in Motion: The Workbook

A Practical Guide to How Religion
Inspires Physical Activity

HEZRON OTTEY

RESOURCE *Publications* · Eugene, Oregon

FAITH IN MOTION: THE WORKBOOK
A Practical Guide to How Religion Inspires Physical Activity

Resource Publications
An Imprint of Wipf and Stock Publishers
199 W. 8th Ave., Suite 3
Eugene, OR 97401

www.wipfandstock.com

PAPERBACK ISBN: 979-8-3852-6354-7
HARDCOVER ISBN: 979-8-3852-6355-4
EBOOK ISBN: 979-8-3852-6356-1

To every believer who has ever felt the gap between what you affirm
with your lips and what you live with your body—
may this be the bridge.
To my family, church, and community—thank you for reminding me
that movement, faith, and love are best lived together.
And to all who are weary yet willing, fragile yet faithful—
this is for you.

For in Him we live and move and have our being.

—Acts 17:28

Contents

Preface

WHAT DOES IT MEAN to truly honor God with our bodies?

That was the question at the heart of my research, my writing, and my own personal journey. As a nurse, a researcher, and a believer, I have sat with countless people of faith who deeply affirmed the value of health—yet struggled to live it. They believed their bodies were temples of the Holy Spirit, but daily life, culture, busyness, shame, and exhaustion often kept them from moving, resting, and worshiping through their physical selves.

This question became the heartbeat of my PhD research. I listened to stories of pastors who preached health but felt trapped in burnout, of mothers who carried guilt for not exercising, of youth who longed for a faith that could move as freely as their bodies did. I witnessed communities where walking together became worship, where laughter on a Sabbath hike turned into healing, where movement restored dignity, resilience, and joy.

From that journey came my book, *Faith in Motion: How Religion Inspires Physical Activity*. But a book, as powerful as it may be, still leaves us with a challenge: How do we move from knowledge to practice? From belief to behavior? From conviction to rhythm?

That is why this workbook exists.

This is not just a companion; it is an invitation. Each page is designed to help you pause, reflect, and step into new rhythms where faith and movement align. Here you will find chapter summaries to keep the vision clear, Scripture anchors to ground your practices, reflection questions that demand honesty, testimonies that remind you that you are not alone, and creative exercises that stretch the imagination as much as the body.

But above all, this workbook is meant to be lived. It will not tell you exactly how many steps to take, how many minutes to stretch, or how many calories to burn. Instead, it will create space for you to discover how God is calling you to embody faith in your own context. Some days you may write.

Some days you may walk. Some days you may simply breathe and rest. And that is enough.

My hope is that this workbook meets you where you are—whether you are a pastor longing for healthier congregations, a student balancing studies and self-care, a parent modelling joy for your children, or an individual carrying both faith and fatigue. Wherever you begin, let this be a companion that reminds you: your body is not an afterthought. It is a temple, testimony, and mission.

The gospel has always been embodied. Jesus walked, touched, healed, and moved among the people. The early disciples spread the good news step by step. And today, your body—your breath, your steps, your stretch—can become part of that same witness.

So, I invite you to journey with me again. Let these pages stir your faith, stretch your imagination, and move your body into alignment with God's grace. And may you discover, as I have, that faith was never meant to sit still.

And neither were you.

Introduction

THIS MORNING, SOMEONE WOKE up and walked the same path to the bus stop they have walked a thousand times. Someone bent down to lift a child into their arms, or to tie their shoes before school. Someone laced up trainers and went for a run. Someone sat in stillness, taking a deep breath before facing another long day.

None of these moments will make the news. None will be posted online. And yet each of them—every step, stretch, breath, or pause—carries within it the possibility of worship.

Faith is not only a set of beliefs stored in the mind or spoken in prayer. It is also something lived with the body. Scripture has always known this. From Abraham setting out on a journey to Jesus walking dusty Galilean roads, faith has pulsed through limbs, breath, sweat, and tears. The story of God's people has never been static—it moves (Acts 17:28).

And that same story is unfolding now, in you.

The tragedy is that modern life has quietly trained us to separate the sacred from the ordinary. We sit in long services, commute in cars, scroll endlessly on screens, and call this "normal." Movement becomes invisible. Health feels optional. Bodies are often treated as problems to be solved rather than vessels of worship and witness.

But the gospel tells a different story. You are not simply a mind that thinks about God or a voice that prays to Him—you are a body designed to carry His presence into the world. In Christ, the body is not a liability. It is testimony. It is temple (1 Cor 6:19–20). It is mission.

Modern research now confirms what Scripture has proclaimed all along—that movement and faith are deeply intertwined. Neuroscientists note that "embodied practices" such as walking, stretching, or rhythmic breathing help regulate the nervous system and deepen memory consolidation.[1] Psychologists observe that physical activity reduces anxiety and depression while strengthening resilience.[2] Public health studies show that group-based walking, dancing, or fitness programs improve not only physical health but also community belonging.[3]

I wrote *Faith in Motion* because I began to notice what happens when this truth is reclaimed. I saw women on evening walks praying aloud for their neighbors. I watched young people bring Scripture alive through dance and rhythm. I sat with men who, through simple daily steps, discovered healing from shame and chronic illness. I listened as families told me that shared hikes and walks restored their communication, laughter, and faith.

These were not just exercises. They were living liturgies—sermons preached with feet, prayers whispered through breath, praise offered in laughter and sweat.

This workbook is designed to help you enter into that same reality. It is not another health plan or productivity tool. It is a companion for transformation. A guide to reframe the motions of your daily life as sacred. A space where you can write, reflect, and act on what it means to honor God with your body—not in theory, but in practice.

Inside, you will find the following:

- Chapter summaries that distill the heartbeat of *Faith in Motion*
- Scripture anchors that tie every practice to the word
- Personal and group reflections to make space for honesty
- "Faith in Action" steps that turn conviction into habit
- Case insights—real testimonies of lives changed by movement
- Creative engagements that invite you to sketch, map, write, or imagine new rhythms
- Closing reflections and prayers to carry forward into your daily routines

This workbook is for the pastor who longs to see a healthier, more vibrant congregation. It is for the student struggling to balance studies, spirituality, and self-care. It is for parents who feel stretched thin and want to model joy

---

1. Van der Kolk, *Body Keeps the Score.*
2. World Health Organization, "Physical Activity."
3. Eime et al., "Systematic Review."

to their children. It is for the weary, the hopeful, the strong, the fragile. It is for everybody—because every body tells a story.

And here is the invitation: let your story be one of faith in motion.

Take this as your moment to pause. Breathe. Write. Stretch. Pray. Then take your first step—not just into the workbook, but into a renewed way of being.

Because faith was never meant to sit still. And neither were you.

HOW TO USE THIS WORKBOOK

Think of this workbook as a journey, not a checklist. It is designed to move with you—through your thoughts, your prayers, your body, and your daily life. Each chapter flows in a rhythm, giving you space to listen, reflect, act, and create.

Here's the simple pattern you'll see again and again:

1. Chapter Summary

A snapshot of the key themes from *Faith in Motion*. This will remind you of the main heartbeat of the chapter, making the big ideas simple and accessible.

2. Scripture Focus

Here you'll find a few carefully chosen verses. These are not for rushing through. Sit with them. Walk with them. Write them down. Let them shape how you see your body, your faith, and your daily rhythms.

3. Reflection

This is where things get personal. You'll find both *personal prompts* (questions just for you) and *group prompts* (if you're working through this with others). Leave space for honesty. There are no "right answers," only real ones.

4. Faith in Action

Here you'll take what you've read and turn it into small, intentional practices. Think of them as experiments—ways to live out what you're learning in your body and in your daily life.

5. Case Insight

You'll encounter stories, testimonies, and voices that bring the themes to life. These are drawn from lived experiences and research. They remind us: we are not alone in this journey.

6. Creative Engagement

Faith is not just about thinking—it is about imagination. In these sections, you'll be invited to draw, map, journal, or move as a way of processing. Use this space to be free, playful, and expressive.

7. Closing Reflection

Each chapter ends with a "heartbeat"—a chance to gather what you've learned into prayer, commitment, or a final thought. This is where you pause before taking your next step.

A gentle reminder: this is *your* workbook. You don't need to fill every line, complete every task, or rush through the chapters. Let the Spirit set the pace. Some days you'll write. Other days you'll walk. Some weeks you may linger on one question, and that's OK.

The goal is not perfection. The goal is presence.

So, grab a pen. Keep this book nearby—on your desk, in your bag, by your Bible. Let it become a companion to your prayers, your movements, your worship, and your growth.

Above all, let it remind you that *faith is not static. It moves. And so do you.*

Chapter 1: Why This Book Matters

(Sections A and B: "Living Temples—The Story Behind the Research" and "Bridging Belief and Behavior—An Invitation to Reimagine Health")

CHAPTER SUMMARY

THIS OPENING CHAPTER INTRODUCES the central question of *Faith in Motion*: What does it mean to live as if our bodies are temples of the Holy Spirit (1 Cor 6:19)? Adventism is globally known for its health message—blue zone communities like Loma Linda have become models of long life and lifestyle discipline. Yet the research revealed a gap between message and motion: while diet and abstinence are often emphasized, physical activity is rarely discussed, preached, or practiced with consistency.

Through lived experiences, Dr. Ottey's research uncovered both barriers and opportunities:

- A grieving widow who stopped walking when life became too heavy
- A mother of three who carried guilt for not exercising, despite believing in the health message
- A pastor who preaches health but neglects his own due to exhaustion
- A young man inspired by his marathon-running pastor
- A walking group that became ministry, evangelism, and fellowship

This is the *embodiment gap*: the distance between what believers affirm and what they live out. Behavioral science and theology agree—information alone does not change lives. Culture, leadership, support systems, and internal motivation all matter.

The invitation of this chapter is not to guilt, but to grace. Movement is not perfectionism; it is participation. The temple isn't abstract. It's your body. And movement is worship.

> *Belief is not the issue. Behavior is not the sole issue either. The issue is alignment. We must align what we preach with what we practice, and what we believe with how we move.*[1]

SCRIPTURE FOCUS

- *1 Cor 6:19–20*—"Do you not know that your body is the temple of the Holy Spirit . . . ? Therefore glorify God in your body."
- *Gen 2:7*—"Then the LORD God formed man of the dust of the ground, and breathed into his nostrils the breath of life."
- *Rom 12:1*—"Present your bodies a living sacrifice, holy, acceptable to God, which is your reasonable service."
- *Mic 6:8*—"What does the LORD require of you but to do justly, to love mercy, and to walk humbly with your God?"

✎ *Underline the verse that speaks most deeply to you. Write why it matters to you today:*

REFLECTION

Personal Reflection

1. How do you currently view your body: as burden, tool, vessel, or temple? Why?

✎ _____

_____

_____

_____

_____

---

1. Ottey, *Faith in Motion*, 12–13.

2. Where do you see the embodiment gap in your own life—between what you believe and what you live?

✎ _____

_____

_____

_____

3. When have you experienced movement (walking, stretching, exercise, dance) as a form of worship or prayer?

✎ _____

_____

_____

_____

Group Reflection

1. Why do you think your church might emphasize diet more than physical activity?

(Group notes) _____

_____

_____

_____

_____

2. What barriers—cultural, emotional, or practical—keep people in your church from being physically active?

(Group notes) _____

_____

_____

_____

_____

3. How might pastors, priests, and leaders model health in ways that encourage congregations?

(Group notes) _____

_____

_____

_____

_____

FAITH IN ACTION: BRIDGING BELIEF AND BEHAVIOR

Temple Walk Practice

- Choose one walk this week and dedicate it to God. Before setting out, pray, "Lord, I honor You with this body and this movement."

- Afterward, write how your spirit responded:

✎ _____

_____

_____

_____

_____

Seven-Day Embodiment Tracker

Record how you honor God with your body each day.

Day	Activity	Duration	How Did I Feel Spiritually?
Mon			
Tue			
Wed			
Thu			

Day	Activity	Duration	How Did I Feel Spiritually?
Fri			
Sat			
Sun			

Community Challenge

Invite one person to join you in movement this week (walking, stretching, gardening, or light exercise). Record what happened:

✎ _____

_____

_____

_____

_____

CASE INSIGHT

> *I believe in the health message. I teach my kids to eat well. But between work, home, and church commitments, I can't find time to exercise. And when I don't, I feel guilty—like I'm failing spiritually."*
> —Mother of three[2]

Reflection Prompt: When has guilt shaped your health practices? What might shift if you reframed movement as grace instead of obligation?

✎ _____

_____

_____

_____

_____

2. Ottey, *Faith in Motion*, 3–4.

CREATIVE ENGAGEMENT

Embodiment Gap Mapping

- On the left, write *What I Believe*. On the right, *What I Live*. Draw arrows to show areas needing alignment.

Draw and Reflect

- Sketch your body (simple outline or stick figure).

- Inside, write one word describing how you see your body now.

- Around the outside, write words that describe how God sees your body.

Liturgical Movement Prayer

- Choose a movement (kneeling, bowing, stretching, walking).

- Repeat: "This temple is Yours, Lord."

- Journal: How did the physical action change your prayer?

_____

_____

_____

_____

_____

_____

_____

_____

_____

CLOSING REFLECTION

The Adventist health message is both a gift and a responsibility. But it is not meant to produce guilt. It is meant to draw us into alignment with God's grace.

Your body is not a metaphor. It is God's temple.

Health is not about perfection—it is about participation.

Every breath, step, and stretch can be an act of worship.

Guided Prayer

- Lord, I thank You for my body because . . .

_____

_____

_____

_____

- Help me to honor You by . . .

_____

_____

_____

- This week, I will live as a temple by . . .

_____

_____

_____

_____

Chapter 2: Faith in Everyday Motion

(Sections A and B: "The Rhythm of Belief in Daily Life" and "From Rhythm to Routine—Integrating Faith and Movement in Real Life")

CHAPTER SUMMARY

This chapter explores how faith is not confined to church pews but is lived out in *everyday motion.* In the ordinary acts of life—walking, bending, lifting, caregiving—there is sacred meaning. "In Him we live and move and have our being" (Acts 17:28).

Interviews with SDA members revealed a tension: the frequent refrain, "*I know, but . . .*"

- "I know my body is a temple, but I don't have time."

- "I know I should move more, but I'm exhausted."

This is not disbelief but the *strain between conviction and constraint.* Some, like Josephine and her "walk and word" group in Birmingham, have reframed walking as devotion and fellowship. But for many, daily movement remains invisible, undervalued, or disconnected from faith.

The chapter also unpacks

- how *domestic motion* (especially by women) is often dismissed as "not exercise";

- the *biblical vision* of walking and discipleship as embodied;

- the *Sabbath paradox*, where rest is equated with stillness instead of restorative motion;

- the *cultural dynamics* of African-Caribbean and African Adventist members, where modesty, survival-driven exercise, or safety concerns shape practices;

- how church culture itself often reinforces sedentariness through long services and meetings.

Section B offers practical pathways: leadership modelling, family integration, congregational rhythms, community outreach, devotional embodiment, and myth-busting reframes. The message is simple but profound: faith is not static—it moves.

> *Faith in motion is Sabbath in your steps. It's theology in your thighs. It's witness in your walk. . . . Every step taken in faith is a sermon.*[1]

SCRIPTURE FOCUS

- *Acts 17:28*—"In Him we live and move and have our being."

- *1 Cor 10:31*—"Whatever you do, do all to the glory of God."

- *Luke 24:15*—"So it was, while they conversed and reasoned, that Jesus Himself drew near and went with them."

- *Gen 5:24*—"Enoch walked with God."

Which verse speaks most to your current daily routine? Why?

_____

_____

_____

_____

_____

_____

_____

---

1. Ottey, *Faith in Motion*, 28.

REFLECTION

Personal Reflection

1. Where in your daily life are you already moving (chores, caregiving, commuting) that you haven't counted as sacred?

_____

_____

_____

_____

_____

2. What cultural or personal messages have shaped your understanding of what "counts" as exercise?

_____

_____

_____

_____

_____

3. How do you view Sabbath movement? Stillness only, or restorative balance?

_____

_____

_____

_____

_____

Group Reflection

1. What unspoken "invisible curriculum" does our church teach about health and movement through our habits and routines?

(Group notes) _____

_____

_____

_____

_____

_____

2. How do leaders' examples shape members' approaches to health?

(Group notes) _____

_____

_____

_____

_____

_____

3. What would our congregation look like if motion was normalized as worship and fellowship?

(Group notes) _____

_____

_____

_____

_____

_____

FAITH IN ACTION: EVERYDAY PRACTICES

Daily Motion Awareness Log (Seven Days)

Use this table to track ordinary motion and reframe it as sacred.

Day	Movements I Did (chores, walking, caregiving)	How I Reframed It as Worship	How I Felt Afterward
Mon			
Tue			
Wed			
Thu			
Fri			
Sat			
Sun			

Family or Group Challenge

- Choose one activity to "reframe" together this week (cooking, cleaning, walking). Pray before starting and dedicate it to God. Reflect after:

✎ _____

_____

_____

_____

_____

Sabbath Reframe Exercise

- Plan one restorative Sabbath motion practice: a nature walk, stretch devotion, or "walk and wonder" with Scripture. Record what you noticed:

✎ _____

_____

_____

_____

_____

_____

_____

CASE INSIGHT

> *My whole life is movement... sweeping, cleaning, walking to the school, bending, lifting. But it doesn't count, right? It's not exercise. It's just life.*
> —Mother of four[2]

Reflection Prompt: How might your perspective change if you recognized ordinary movements as valid, sacred stewardship?

✎ _____

_____

_____

_____

_____

_____

_____

2. Ottey, *Faith in Motion*, 16.

CREATIVE ENGAGEMENT

Invisible to Sacred Mapping

- List five "invisible" movements you already do.

- Next to each, write how you might reframe it as worship.

Example:

- Washing dishes → *Cleansing and gratitude prayer*

Draw and Imagine

- Sketch your weekly routine. Circle one place where you can insert sacred movement.

Liturgical Experiment

- Try a "verse and move" practice this week (e.g., stretch with Ps 23, walk with Mic 6:8).

- Journal what shifts in your spirit:

✎ _____

_____

_____

_____

CLOSING REFLECTION

Faith was never meant to sit still. From Abraham to Jesus to the disciples, the story of God's people is a story of walking, moving, living theology.

Your body's movements—seen and unseen, ordinary and extraordinary— are all sites of worship when aligned with faith.

Every breath, step, and chore can become an act of devotion. Every walk can become a pilgrimage. Every stretch can become a psalm.

Guided Prayer

- Lord, thank You for the movements I already make . . .

_____

_____

- Help me to see daily routines as sacred by . . .

_____

_____

- This week, I will honor You in my body by . . .

_____

_____

Chapter 3: Leadership in Motion

(Sections A and B: "The Influence of Embodied Leadership" and "Cultivating a Culture of Movement in Church Leadership and Congregational Life")

CHAPTER SUMMARY

Leadership in the Seventh-day Adventist Church is more than preaching or policy—it is embodied influence. Members watch not only what leaders say, but how they live. A pastor's walk, an elder's meal choices, a director's approach to rest—they all become part of the message.

In research interviews, participants highlighted both inspiration and disillusionment:

- A pastor who led weekly walks inspired members to value health.

- Elders' sedentary habits sent the opposite message.

- One elder observed, "You can't preach temperance from a place of burnout."[1]

This chapter names the silent sermon of leadership habits: walking breaks, Sabbath rhythms, prayer walks, honest testimonies, and self-care. It also addresses barriers—time pressure, cultural expectations, guilt, and lack of support—that prevent leaders from embodying health.

Section B expands the vision: leadership must not only inspire but also cultivate a culture of movement. From worship to board meetings, potlucks to Sabbath services, health is not a program but an ecosystem. When leaders

---

1. Ottey, *Faith in Motion*, 30.

model motion, embed it into systems, redesign worship practices, and re-imagine Health Ministries, churches begin to breathe wholeness.

The call is not perfection but alignment: leaders who embody health create congregations that follow.

> The world does not need more eloquent sermons. It needs visible lives of wholeness, humility, and embodied grace.[2]

SCRIPTURE FOCUS

- *Matt 5:16*—"Let your light so shine before men, that they may see your good works and glorify your Father in heaven."

- *1 Cor 6:19–20*—"Do you not know that your body is the temple of the Holy Spirit . . . ? Therefore glorify God in your body."

- *Exod 18:17–18*—"The thing that you do is not good. Both you and these people who are with you will surely wear yourselves out. For this thing is too much for you; you are not able to perform it by yourself."

- *Heb 13:7*—"Remember those who rule over you, who have spoken the word of God to you, whose faith follow, considering the outcome of their conduct."

Which verse speaks most strongly to your picture of leadership right now?

✎ _____

_____

_____

_____

_____

_____

_____

_____

2. Ottey, *Faith in Motion*, 34.

REFLECTION

Personal Reflection (for Leaders and Members)

1. In what ways does my current lifestyle model (or not model) the Adventist health message?

_____

_____

_____

_____

2. Am I leading from overflow or depletion? How would I know the difference?

_____

_____

_____

_____

3. How do my habits around rest, movement, and nourishment affect my ministry and family?

_____

_____

_____

_____

Group Reflection

1. What silent sermons are our leaders preaching through their habits of rest, health, and movement?

(Group notes) _____

_____

_____

_____

2. How does our church culture support—or undermine—leader health?

(Group notes) _____

_____

_____

_____

3. What small, symbolic practices could our leadership team begin (e.g., prayer walks, standing devotions, wellness check-ins)?

(Group notes) _____

_____

_____

_____

FAITH IN ACTION: EMBODIED LEADERSHIP PRACTICES

Leadership Health Tracker (Seven Days)

Day	My Movement (walk, stretch, rest)	Did I Model It Visibly?	Impact on Energy/ Spirit
Mon			
Tue			
Wed			
Thu			
Fri			
Sat			
Sun			

Team Challenge

This week, suggest one health-based adjustment at a meeting (e.g., a stretch break, a walking agenda item). Record what happened:

✎ _____

_____

_____

_____

Family/Ministry Integration

Plan one "visible health practice" that members can see (e.g., Sabbath walk, posting reflections from a daily walk, sharing personal testimony of rest). What did you notice about how people responded?

✎ _____

_____

_____

_____

CASE INSIGHT

> *Our previous pastor led a weekly walking group. He didn't talk about health every Sabbath, but you knew it mattered to him. And that made me want to care about it more too.*
> —Research participant[3]

Reflection Prompt: Think of a leader (pastor, elder, parent, mentor) who inspired you by embodying their values. What did they model? How did it affect you?

✎ _____

_____

_____

_____

_____

3. Ottey, *Faith in Motion*, 30.

CREATIVE ENGAGEMENT

Silent Sermon Mapping

- Draw two columns: "What I Say" and "What I Do."

- Fill in examples of your leadership habits. Circle one area where your actions already align with your words, and one area needing growth.

Design a Culture Shift

- Sketch or outline what a Sabbath service in your church might look like if motion was naturally included (walking liturgy, stretch and Scripture, outdoor prayer circles).

Embodied Prayer Practice

- Try leading (or personally practicing) a "walk and reflect" devotion this week:

    1. Read Matt 5:16.

    2. Walk slowly for ten minutes, repeating, *"Let my life be light."*

    3. Journal your experience:

_____

_____

_____

_____

_____

_____

_____

_____

CLOSING REFLECTION

Leadership is influence—but it is also embodiment. When leaders rest, walk, stretch, or model balance, they are not indulging the flesh but investing in the future of the church.

The pulpit is not the only platform. The body of the leader is also a pulpit. And the world listens.

> *Let the leader walk first. . . . Because when leadership moves with grace, the whole body begins to move toward health.*[4]

---

4. Ottey, *Faith in Motion*, 36.

Guided Prayer for Leaders and Members

- Lord, thank You for the leaders who have modelled wholeness in my life:

_____

_____

_____

_____

_____

_____

- Help me to lead (or support leaders) with integrity of word and body by . . .

_____

_____

_____

_____

_____

_____

- This week, may I shine light through action by . . .

_____

_____

_____

_____

_____

_____

Chapter 4: Barriers and Breakthroughs

(Sections A and B: "Naming the Real-World Obstacles to Physical Activity in Faith Communities" and "Pathways to Breakthrough—Redefining the Health Message with Grace, Grit, and Community")

CHAPTER SUMMARY

This chapter names the barriers to movement that many Seventh-day Adventists face—not as excuses, but as invitations. The gap between theology and practice is shaped by real challenges:

- *Time poverty*: overcommitment to family, work, and church duties

- *Cultural expectations*: especially gendered roles that prize service over self-care

- *Safety and environment*: unsafe streets, lack of green space, pollution

- *Fatigue and burnout*: spiritual and emotional depletion that steals energy

- *Shame and comparison*: fear of judgment or feeling "unfit" for movement

- *Theological misunderstandings*: beliefs that Sabbath prohibits activity, or that exercise is vain

Yet in every barrier lies the seed of breakthrough. Section B reframes health as discipleship, promotes small steps with sacred intent, calls for inclusive spaces, champions movement as ministry, and points to leadership, Sabbath, storytelling, and structural support as pathways to grace-filled embodiment.

> *The barriers are real. But so is the breakthrough. Movement is not just possible—it is promised, when we move with the Spirit.*[1]

SCRIPTURE FOCUS

- *Matt 26:41*—"The spirit indeed is willing, but the flesh is weak."

- *Isa 40:31*—"Those who wait on the Lord shall renew their strength; . . . they shall run and not be weary, they shall walk and not faint."

- *1 Pet 5:10*—"After you have suffered a while, [the God of all grace will] perfect, establish, strengthen, and settle you."

Which verse feels most relevant to your current struggles with health or movement? Why?

✎ _____

_____

_____

_____

REFLECTION

Personal Reflection

1. Which of the barriers named (time poverty, fatigue, shame, culture, safety, theology) resonates most with your experience?

✎ _____

_____

_____

_____

---

1. Ottey, *Faith in Motion*, 51.

2. What emotions do you feel when you think about physical activity: guilt, joy, fear, duty, gratitude? Why?

✎ _____

_____

_____

_____

3. Where have you experienced a breakthrough—however small—in your health journey?

✎ _____

_____

_____

_____

Group Reflection

1. What barriers seem most common in our congregation?

(Group notes) _____

_____

_____

_____

_____

2. How has our church unintentionally reinforced these barriers (through routines, expectations, or silence)?

(Group notes) _____

_____

_____

_____

_____

3. What breakthroughs have we seen together that could be celebrated and built upon?

(Group notes) _____

_____

_____

_____

_____

_____

FAITH IN ACTION: FROM NAMING TO MOVING

Barrier Awareness Journal

Each day, identify one barrier you face and reframe it with grace.

Day	Barrier I Noticed	My Reframe	My Next Step
Mon			
Tue			
Wed			
Thu			
Fri			
Sat			
Sun			

Micro-Practices for Breakthroughs

Try one small practice this week:

- Two to five minutes of stretching after prayer

- A gratitude walk around the block

- Chair stretches during meetings

- Pair one Scripture verse with one motion (e.g., breathe deeply with Ps 46:10)

Record your experience:

✎ _____

_____

_____

_____

_____

_____

_____

Congregational Idea

Suggest a small breakthrough practice your church could adopt (e.g., standing devotions, post-service walks, intergenerational step challenges).

✎ _____

_____

_____

_____

_____

_____

_____

CASE INSIGHT

I'm always doing something—for the kids, the church, my job. If I sit down to rest, I feel guilty. And exercise? That's a luxury I can't afford.
—Youth Director, South England[2]

Reflection Prompt: How does guilt show up in your approach to health? What would change if you saw movement as sacred investment rather than selfish indulgence?

✎ _____

_____

_____

_____

_____

_____

CREATIVE ENGAGEMENT

Barrier Mapping Exercise

- Draw a circle with the word *Movement* in the middle.

- Around it, write your barriers (time, fatigue, shame, etc.).

- Draw arrows showing small possible breakthroughs.

---

2. Ottey, *Faith in Motion*, 46.

Reframing Myths

Rewrite these common myths with truth:

- "Exercise is secular." →_____

_____

- "Sabbath is for sitting." →_____

_____

- "I don't have time." →_____

_____

Embodied Breakthrough Prayer

- Choose a posture (walking, stretching, kneeling).

- Pray Isa 40:31 aloud as you move.

- Journal what you experienced:

✎ _____

_____

_____

_____

_____

_____

CLOSING REFLECTION

Barriers are real. But they are not the end of the story. In every weight of time poverty, fatigue, shame, or misunderstanding, God's Spirit whispers renewal. Breakthroughs rarely come through pressure or performance. They emerge through grace, grit, and community.

The invitation is simple: one step, one breath, one act of reframing. From shame to grace. From depletion to renewal. From isolation to fellowship.

> *The breakthrough begins with one step. Let us walk in faith. Let us move in grace. Let us become the body of Christ—in motion.*[3]

Guided Prayer

- Lord, the barrier I most struggle with is . . .

_____

_____

_____

_____

- Teach me to reframe it with Your grace by . . .

_____

_____

_____

_____

- This week, I will take one step toward breakthrough by . . .

_____

_____

_____

_____

3. Ottey, *Faith in Motion*, 58.

Chapter 5: The Role of Community in Sustaining Motion

(Sections A and B: "Faith, Fellowship, and the Power of Collective Movement" and "Building Systems That Carry Movement Across Generations")

CHAPTER SUMMARY

If movement begins with individual intention, it is sustained by *community*. The Seventh-day Adventist Church is a body designed to gather, share, and serve together—yet many members struggle alone with their health. This chapter reframes community as the essential environment where movement becomes shared joy rather than solitary discipline.

Section A explores the following:

- *The theology of togetherness*: walking, fellowship, and discipleship as embodied and communal

- *Social support* as a strong predictor of sustained health habits

- *The ministry of presence*: showing up to walk with someone, carry water, or simply accompany them

- *Faith-based identity and celebration*: movement as part of Adventist identity, reinforced through rituals, visuals, and testimonies

- *Overcoming isolation* by intentionally including seniors, those with chronic illness, or those struggling with mental health

- *Intergenerational integration*: normalizing movement across ages so that walking, stretching, and celebrating become part of heritage

Section B moves from inspiration to *systems that last.* It covers the following:

- Institutionalizing health without bureaucracy

- Embedding movement in the church calendar

- Cross-ministry collaboration

- Designing spaces that preach motion

- Training new leaders and passing health practices across generations

- Funding, measuring, and sustaining health with resilience

- Building a "movement liturgy" where even worship services embed embodied practices

The chapter concludes that *systems are sacred.* To sustain movement is to leave a legacy for the next generation.

> *A movement without structure is a moment. But a movement with structure becomes a legacy.*[1]

SCRIPTURE FOCUS

- *Heb 10:24–25*—"And let us consider one another in order to stir up love and good works, not forsaking the assembling of ourselves together, . . . but exhorting one another."

- *Eccl 4:9–10*—"Two are better than one. . . . If they fall, one will lift up his companion."

- *Hab 2:2*—"Write the vision and make it plain . . . that he may run who reads it."

---

1. Ottey, *Faith in Motion*, 67.

Which verse speaks most to your experience of community and health right now?

✎ _____

_____

_____

_____

_____

REFLECTION

Personal Reflection

1. Who in your life helps you move, walk, or live healthier? How do they encourage you?

✎ _____

_____

_____

_____

_____

2. Have you ever felt isolated in your health journey? What emotions came with that?

✎ _____

_____

_____

_____

_____

3. How does your church currently celebrate or neglect physical health in community life?

✎ _____

_____

_____

_____

Group Reflection

1. Where does our congregation already embody togetherness in health?

(Group notes) _____

_____

_____

_____

2. What barriers keep some members excluded from health practices?

(Group notes) _____

_____

_____

_____

3. What systems or rituals could we add to normalize motion across ministries?

(Group notes) _____

_____

_____

_____

FAITH IN ACTION: MOVING TOGETHER

Buddy System Log

Find a movement buddy this week. Write their name and the practice you'll share.

Buddy's Name	What We Did	How It Felt Spiritually

Family/Group Challenge

Choose one collective activity (e.g., Sabbath walk, stretching before a meal, family dance to praise music). Reflect:

✎ _____

_____

_____

_____

_____

_____

_____

Church-Wide Micro-Practices

- Add two minutes of "Stretch and Scripture" between Sabbath school and divine service.

- Share health testimonies once a month.

- Start a WhatsApp group for encouragement and daily step logs.

- Celebrate one small health victory at every board meeting.

Which one could you pilot in your church this month?

✎ _____

_____

_____

_____

_____

_____

CASE INSIGHT

*My neighbor walks with me every Friday. We don't talk about
fitness. We talk about life. But I move because she comes.*
—Participant, West Midlands[2]

Reflection Prompt: Who could you simply "show up for" in your health
journey—or who could show up for you?

✎ _____

_____

_____

_____

_____

CREATIVE ENGAGEMENT

Community Web Mapping

- Draw your name in the center.

- Around it, add names of people who could support your health.

- Draw lines to show existing connections and dotted lines for ones
  you want to build.

2. Ottey, *Faith in Motion*, 62.

Movement Liturgy Design

Sketch or write how your church service could include movement naturally: standing benedictions, walking prayers, body psalms.

Celebration Vision Board

Cut or draw images/words that represent how your community could celebrate health—certificates, Temple Walks, murals, testimonies. Paste/assemble as a vision for collective culture.

CLOSING REFLECTION

Community is the container for sustainable health. Together, we reduce shame, overcome isolation, and create joy. Systems help ensure that what starts as a moment becomes a movement, passed from generation to generation.

The gospel was never meant to stand still. Neither were we.[3]

Guided Prayer

- Lord, thank You for the people who walk beside me:

_____

_____

_____

_____

- Help me to build systems of health in my community by . . .

_____

_____

_____

_____

- This week, let me take one step toward collective movement by . . .

_____

_____

_____

_____

3. Ottey, *Faith in Motion*, 66.

Chapter 6: Movement as Mission—Witnessing Through the Way We Live

(Sections A and B: "Embodied Testimony in the Public Square" and "Mobilizing the Church—Models and Strategies for Movement-Based Ministry")

CHAPTER SUMMARY

Movement is not only health—it is *mission*. The Adventist health message, when embodied and visible, becomes public witness. To walk joyfully, stretch openly, and live energetically is to preach the gospel with our bodies.

Section A explores the following:

- Movement as public testimony—visible, joyful, missional

- Walking as biblical witness: pilgrimage, discipleship, accessibility

- Serving the marginalized through embodied ministry

- Evangelism reimagined as presence, not just proclamation

- The church as a "city on a hill" that must not stand still

Section B provides practical models for making this real:

- *The Walking Church* (pilgrimage-style outreach)

- *Move and Serve Events* (physical activity + service)

- *Health Hubs on the Move* (public wellness + prayer presence)

- *Movement as Discipleship Pathways* (embodied devotions, Psalms walks, health-linked baptism prep)

- Strategies for embedding movement into worship, communications, digital platforms, and church culture

- Case studies like *Temple Trek* in South Yorkshire, where intergenerational congregations walked, worshiped, and witnessed together

The conclusion reminds us: *mission begins with a step.* Every body in motion is a sermon.

SCRIPTURE FOCUS

- *Matt 5:16*—"Let your light so shine before men, that they may see your good works and glorify your Father in heaven."

- *Phil 4:9*—"The things which you learned and received and heard and saw in me, these do."

- *Matt 5:14*—"You are the light of the world. A city that is set on a hill cannot be hidden."

Which Scripture do you most connect with when you think about health as mission? Why?

✎ _____

_____

_____

_____

_____

_____

_____

_____

_____

REFLECTION

Personal Reflection

1. How visible is your health journey to others right now?

✎ _____

_____

_____

2. Have you ever seen someone's health or vitality inspire curiosity about their faith? What happened?

✎ _____

_____

_____

3. How comfortable are you with your body being part of your witness?

✎ _____

_____

_____

Group Reflection

1. What public spaces near our church could become mission grounds for movement (parks, schools, markets)?

(Group notes) _____

_____

2. What fears or hesitations might members have about public witness through health?

(Group notes) _____

_____

3. What opportunities already exist for us to blend movement and mission?

(Group notes) _____

_____

FAITH IN ACTION: MODELS FOR MISSIONAL MOVEMENT

Try One Model This Month

Pick one of the four models from chapter 6 and outline your plan:

Model	First Step I'll Take	Who Will Join Me?	When?
Walking Church			
Move and Serve			
Health Hub			
Discipleship Pathway			

Micro-Practices for Public Witness

- Wear Scripture on your walk (T-shirt, badge, tote bag).

- Take a five-minute "neighborhood blessing walk."

- Share one health reflection on social media tied to faith.

- Invite a friend or colleague for a walk-and-talk with prayer.

✎ Which one will you start this week?

CASE INSIGHT

In Birmingham, a congregation launched "Gospel on the Go." . . .
Within weeks, shop owners began offering water, residents asked to
join, and teens began engaging with the group.[1]

Reflection Prompt: What small act of public witness could your church
start that would naturally invite community curiosity?

✎ _____

CREATIVE ENGAGEMENT

Movement Mission Map

Draw a map of your neighborhood. Mark the following:

- Where your church gathers

- Where people naturally move (parks, schools, high streets)

- Potential prayer/movement stations

Plan a "movement route" with three to five stops for reflection, prayer, or
service.

---

1. Ottey, *Faith in Motion*, 78.

Design Your Own Campaign

Brainstorm a movement campaign for your church:

- Title: _____

- Key verse: _____

- Core activity (walk, run, stretch, serve): _____

- Community invitation: _____

- Celebration element: _____

Embodied Prayer

Practice a "Prayer Walk Liturgy":

- Step 1: Begin with thanksgiving.

- Step 2: Walk slowly, praying for neighbors.

- Step 3: Pause at a landmark—pray for that institution.

- Step 4: Return giving thanks.

Record your experience:

✎ _____

_____

_____

_____

_____

_____

_____

_____

_____

_____

CLOSING REFLECTION

Mission begins with a step. A moving church is a visible church. A body that walks in grace becomes a sermon the world can see. From high streets to hillsides, from neighborhoods to nations, when Adventists embody their faith through health, they bear a gospel of joy, vitality, and hope.

Your body, in motion, is a message. Let it be read with joy.[2]

Guided Prayer

- Lord, show me where my steps can carry Your message.

- Give me courage to witness with my body, not just my words.

- Let our church become a community in motion, visible with grace, alive with hope.

2. Ottey, *Faith in Motion*, 81.

Chapter 7: Reclaiming the Body— Faith, Movement, and the Sacred Self

(Sections A and B: "The Theology of the Body Reimagined" and "Embodied Disciplines—Practicing Faith Through Movement")

CHAPTER SUMMARY

This chapter reclaims a biblical vision of the body as sacred. Scripture and the incarnation remind us that our bodies are not burdens but vessels of the Spirit. We explore how embodiment reflects God's design, how Sabbath restores body and spirit, how Jesus Himself moved with compassion, and how worship is full-bodied. We also confront shame, replacing it with joy and freedom in motion.

Section B introduces embodied disciplines—walking, stretching, breath prayer, sacred dance, fasting with intention, stillness, and embodied intercession. These practices remind us that faith is not only spoken or thought, but lived in every breath, step, and gesture.

The central message is this: *your body is God's temple—move like it, rest like it, pray like it.*

SCRIPTURE FOCUS

- *1 Cor 6:19-20*—"Do you not know that your body is the temple of the Holy Spirit . . . ? Therefore glorify God in your body."

- *Rom 12:1*—"Present your bodies a living sacrifice, holy, acceptable to God, which is your reasonable service."

- *Ps 150:6*—"Let everything that has breath praise the LORD."

- *John 1:14*—"The Word became flesh and dwelt among us."

Which verse most challenges your current view of your body? Why?

✎ _____

_____

_____

_____

_____

_____

REFLECTION

Personal Reflection

1. Have you ever viewed your body as a liability instead of a gift? What shaped that view?

✎ _____

_____

2. Where do you most feel God's presence—stillness, walking, dancing, resting?

✎ _____

_____

3. How does shame or cultural expectation influence how you move or worship?

✎ _____

_____

Group Reflection

1. What messages does our church culture send (spoken or unspoken) about the body?

(Group notes) _____

_____

2. How might integrating movement into worship change our communal life?

(Group notes) _____

_____

3. What practices of embodied faith could we model to counter shame and celebrate joy?

(Group notes) _____

_____

FAITH IN ACTION: EMBODIED PRACTICES

Weekly Embodied Disciplines Tracker

Day	Practice (walk, stretch, breath, dance, rest, intercession)	Scripture Link	Reflection
Mon			
Tue			
Wed			
Thu			
Fri			
Sat			
Sun			

Family or Group Challenge

Try one embodied discipline together this week (e.g., prayer walk, Scripture stretch, or movement worship). Reflect afterwards: How did this deepen our sense of God's presence?

✎ _____

_____

Sabbath Reframe Exercise

Plan a Sabbath rhythm that integrates body and spirit (nature walk, breath circle, or gratitude stretch). Journal what shifted for you:

✎ _____ .

_____

CASE INSIGHT

Jesus didn't just save souls. He restored bodies.[1]

Every miracle story is also a movement story—the paralytic rising, Zacchaeus climbing, Peter stepping out of the boat. Healing was never abstract; it was embodied.

Testimony from a Participant

> *I used to think worship was only about my words. Then I realized— when I lifted my hands, my heart lifted too. When I walked while praying, my mind cleared. When I danced, my shame broke. My body became part of my prayer.*
> —Participant testimony

1. Ottey, *Faith in Motion*, 95.

Reflection Prompt: How might your body become a partner—not a barrier—in your spiritual life?

✎ _____

_____

_____

_____

CREATIVE ENGAGEMENT

Body-as-Temple Map

- Draw an outline of your body. On each part, write one way you can honor God with it (hands for service, feet for walking in faith, lungs for praise, etc.).

Embodied Psalm Practice

- Take Ps 150 and create simple body movements (clap, sway, stretch, kneel) to match each verse. Perform this as a personal or group devotion.

Liberation from Shame Ritual

- Write one negative message you've believed about your body. Then, while walking, stretch your arms wide and pray aloud: "I am fearfully and wonderfully made." Record what you experienced:

✎ _____

_____

_____

CLOSING REFLECTION

The gospel is not disembodied—it is incarnational. Jesus wept, touched, walked, reclined, and rose again in His body. Our own discipleship must reclaim the sacredness of embodiment.

When we stretch, we surrender. When we breathe, we receive grace. When we walk, we journey with God. When we dance, we declare freedom. When we rest, we trust His care.

Your body is not the enemy of faith—it is the stage where redemption unfolds.

Guided Prayer

- Lord, thank You for my body . . .

_____

_____

_____

- Teach me to move in ways that honor You by . . .

_____

_____

_____

- Free me from shame so I can rejoice in . . .

Chapter 8: Healing Through Motion— Restoring the Body, Mind, and Spirit

(Sections A and B: "The Therapeutic Power of Movement" and "Testimonies of Transformation—Stories of Healing in Motion")

CHAPTER SUMMARY

This chapter explores movement as more than discipline or devotion—it is medicine. Motion supports trauma recovery, mental health, grief processing, and the rebuilding of self-worth. It also heals communities and churches, helping us embody resilience and restoration together.

Testimonies reveal how walking, dancing, stretching, and collective action transform lives: Isaac reclaimed hope after depression, Lydia found healing in grief through dance, the Wright family restored their relationships through walking, Riverside SDA reimagined outreach, Daniel rewrote shame into purpose, and youth discovered revival through Scripture in motion.

The message is clear: *movement heals.* Every step, stretch, and breath can become an altar of recovery and a testimony of grace.

SCRIPTURE FOCUS

- *Jer 30:17*—"'I will restore health to you and heal you of your wounds,' says the LORD."

- *Ps 66:5*—"Come and see the works of God; He is awesome in His doing toward the sons of men."

- *1 Pet 5:10*—"May the God of all grace . . . perfect, establish, strengthen, and settle you."

Which of these verses speaks to your own journey of healing? Why?

✏ _____

_____

_____

_____

_____

_____

REFLECTION

Personal Reflection

1. Where have you experienced movement as part of your healing—emotionally, physically, or spiritually?

✏ _____

_____

2. Which barriers (fear, shame, fatigue, grief) have hindered your healing through motion?

✏ _____

_____

3. What step of embodied healing might God be inviting you to take this week?

✏ _____

_____

Group Reflection

1. How could our church become a space of healing through intentional movement?

(Group notes) _____

_____

2. Which community needs (grief, trauma, isolation) could embodied practices help address?

(Group notes) _____

_____

3. What would it look like for us to normalize testimonies of healing in motion alongside other testimonies?

(Group notes) _____

_____

FAITH IN ACTION: PRACTICES FOR HEALING

Healing Movement Log (Seven Days)

Day	Movement Practice (walk, stretch, dance)	Healing Focus (grief, stress, trauma, joy)	Reflection
Mon			
Tue			
Wed			
Thu			
Fri			
Sat			
Sun			

Family or Group Healing Challenge

Choose one healing practice to try together this week (e.g., grief walk, gratitude stretch, or prayer dance). Afterwards, share: What did it unlock for us?

✎ _____

_____

Sabbath Healing Ritual

Design a Sabbath practice of gentle healing motion (e.g., slow walk, candlelit stretch, or breath prayer in community). Record what shifted in your body or spirit.

✎ _____

_____

CASE INSIGHT

Isaac's Revival

"I thought it was just exercise . . . but it became my revival."[1] After daily "Hope Walks," Isaac moved from depression into renewed faith, new work, and mentoring others.

Lydia's Dance

Grieving her mother, Lydia discovered freedom in movement ministry. Dance helped her cry, release, and honor her loss—birthing "Sacred Grief Circles" that now support women across Birmingham.

Reflection Prompt: What testimony from these stories most resonates with your own life? How could your healing journey also become a testimony?

✎ _____

_____

_____

1. Ottey, *Faith in Motion*, 114.

CREATIVE ENGAGEMENT

Healing Map

- Draw your body outline. On it, mark where stress, grief, or fatigue rests. Next, add movements that could release those areas (walk, stretch, sway, breathe).

Grief and Grace Ritual

- Light a candle and walk slowly in silence. With each step, recall a memory or prayer. Write what surfaced:

_____

_____

_____

_____

_____

_____

_____

_____

Testimony Wall

- Write one sentence of embodied healing you've experienced (e.g., "Walking gave me back my peace"). Imagine posting it publicly. What impact might it have on others?

✎ _____

_____

CLOSING REFLECTION

Movement does not erase pain, but it transforms it. In walking, stretching, and dancing, grief becomes bearable, trauma finds release, communities find unity, and bodies recover dignity. Healing is not abstract—it is embodied.

Every step of recovery is sacred. Every breath is a benediction. Every testimony in motion is a witness to God's restoring grace.

Guided Prayer

- Lord, thank You for the ways You bring healing through my body . . .

_____

_____

_____

- Help me to move into wholeness by . . .

_____

_____

_____

- May my testimony in motion inspire others to trust Your restoring power.

Chapter 9: Designing a Movement-Based Ministry—Models, Resources, and Next Steps

(Sections A and B: "Foundations for an Embodied Faith Practice" and "Blueprints for Movement Ministries—Practical Models for Diverse Contexts")

CHAPTER SUMMARY

This chapter moves us from inspiration to design. Testimonies in chapter 8 revealed how healing through motion transforms lives. But to carry that transformation across a congregation or community, we need more than moments—we need ministries.

Section A lays foundations: rooting in theology; assessing readiness; choosing anchors like healing, worship, discipleship, restoration, community, and witness; and forming inclusive leadership teams. Section B provides sample blueprints—walking groups, women's embodied devotion, family events, youth creative projects, church-wide challenges, and health partnerships.

The call is simple: ministries of movement are not side programs. They are part of discipleship. With thoughtful planning and joyful practice, churches can become cultures of embodied faith where every step is worship.

SCRIPTURE FOCUS

- *Col 3:17*—"Whatever you do in word or deed, do all in the name of the Lord Jesus."

- *1 Cor 12:12*—"The body is one and has many members, but all the members of that one body, being many, are one body."

- *Hab 2:2*—"Write the vision and make it plain . . . that he may run who reads it."

Which verse most speaks to your community's next step in building a culture of movement? Why?

✎ _____

_____

_____

_____

REFLECTION

Personal Reflection

1. Where in your own life do you already design structure—work, family, health—that could also apply to ministry planning?

✎ _____

_____

2. What fears might you have about leading or suggesting a movement-based initiative?

✎ _____

_____

3. Which anchor (healing, worship, discipleship, restoration, community, witness) resonates most deeply with your calling?

✎ _____

_____

Group Reflection

1. How does our church currently approach health and embodiment—through sermons, silence, or service?

(Group notes) _____

_____

2. What unspoken barriers (theological, cultural, generational) could hold us back?

(Group notes) _____

_____

3. What would change if health and movement were part of our church calendar and culture every year?

(Group notes) _____

_____

FAITH IN ACTION: DESIGNING STEPS

Movement Ministry Design Tracker

Step	Action	Who Can Help?	Completed (✔)
1	Root in theology (Bible study or sermon series)		
2	Listen (survey or group session)		
3	Choose two to three ministry anchors		
4	Form a small, diverse team		
5	Pilot one small initiative		
6	Collect testimonies and stories		
7	Celebrate and evaluate		

Four-Week Pilot Log

Week	Small Step I Tried	Who Joined Me	What I Learned
1			
2			
3			
4			

Congregational Challenge

Choose one pilot initiative this month:

- A Prayer Walk
- Stretch and Scripture gathering
- Family in Motion Day
- Thirty-Day Step Challenge
- Youth "Verse in Motion" project

Reflect on how people responded:

✎ _____

_____

_____

_____

_____

_____

_____

_____

_____

CASE INSIGHT

Adventist Church—Sacred Steps Challenge

One Adventist Church launched a thirty-day step challenge where each daily step goal was paired with Scripture and a reflection question. By the end of the month, over 80 percent of members had participated, and their closing walkathon became a community event with neighbors and local leaders joining in.
One member testified: "I've never prayed so much while moving."

Reflection Prompt: How could your church use a simple, joyful challenge to bring people together across ages and backgrounds?

✎ _____

_____

_____

_____

_____

_____

CREATIVE ENGAGEMENT

Anchor Mapping

List the three anchors you'd choose for your ministry. Write practices under each.

Example: *Community → weekly prayer walk; Healing → chair stretches; Worship → embodied praise*

Blueprint Sketch

Design a one-month pilot. Write its name, audience, Scripture theme, and key activity.

Embodied Scripture Practice

Read Col 3:17 while standing tall, bowing low, and lifting your hands.

Journal: How did this feel different than just reading silently?

✎ _____

_____

_____

_____

_____

_____

_____

Vision Wall

Sketch or write what a banner saying "We are a moving people" would look like if it hung in your fellowship hall.

CLOSING REFLECTION

Designing a movement ministry is not about adding another program. It is about embedding a culture of embodied discipleship—where the body joins the heart, mind, and soul in worship and witness. Testimonies inspire, but structure sustains. When we plan with prayer, every calendar entry, every stretch, and every step can become worship.

Guided Prayer

- Lord, thank You for giving vision to Your church . . .

_____

_____

_____

- Help me to design simple but lasting ways to honor You in body and spirit by . . .

_____

_____

_____

- May our congregation become a witness of grace in motion by . . .

_____

_____

_____

Chapter 10: Sustaining the Movement—Legacy, Leadership, and Lifelong Impact

(Sections A and B: "From Program to Culture—Embedding Embodied Faith" and "Beyond the Church Walls—Movement as Mission and Public Witness")

CHAPTER SUMMARY

This chapter invites us to think beyond events and projects. Movements are born in moments, but they only last when they grow into cultures. Section A shows how to shift from programs to long-term rhythms: clarifying vision, equipping leaders, embedding movement into church life, celebrating milestones, and adapting through reflection. Section B takes the vision outward—movement as witness in public spaces, as partnership with local institutions, as evangelism, as intercultural practice, and as digital discipleship.

 The heart of sustaining the movement is this: we are not building programs; we are building legacies. A legacy of embodied worship, mission, and healing that future generations inherit and continue.

SCRIPTURE FOCUS

- *Gal 6:9*—"Let us not grow weary while doing good, for in due season we shall reap if we do not lose heart."

- *Isa 52:7*—"How beautiful upon the mountains are the feet of him who brings good news."

- *Acts 17:28*—"In Him we live and move and have our being."

Which of these verses most challenges or encourages you as you think about sustaining embodied faith in your community?

✎ _____

_____

_____

_____

_____

_____

_____

REFLECTION

Personal Reflection

1. What motivates you to keep going when ministry feels tiring?

✎ _____

_____

_____

2. Where do you see potential leaders in your community who could help sustain the work?

✎ _____

_____

_____

3. What fears might hold you back from dreaming long-term?

✎ _____

_____

_____

Group Reflection

1. How does our church currently celebrate health and movement—do we make it visible, or keep it hidden?

(Group notes) _____

_____

2. What would it look like if every ministry (youth, worship, elders, community service) had an embodied dimension?

(Group notes) _____

_____

3. How could we take one part of our embodied faith practices into the public square with integrity and grace?

(Group notes) _____

_____

FAITH IN ACTION: SUSTAINING STEPS

Vision and Culture Tracker

Step	Action	Who Leads?	Progress (✔)
1	Clarify and communicate the "why"		
2	Develop a leadership pipeline		
3	Embed practices into worship/liturgy		
4	Celebrate milestones and testimonies		
5	Evaluate and adapt		

Movement Leadership Development Log

Month	New Leaders Identified	Training Given	Care/Support Provided
Jan			
Feb			
Mar			
Apr			
May			
June			
July			
Aug			
Sept			
Oct			
Nov			
Dec			

Community Challenge

Choose one way to carry movement beyond your church walls this month:

- Prayer Walk in neighborhoods
- Healing Circle in a community center
- Family "Faith and Motion" pop-up in a park
- Digital "Move and Meditate" devotional online

What happened when you tried it?

✎ _____

_____

_____

_____

_____

_____

_____

_____

_____

_____

CASE INSIGHT

Hope SDA—"Bless This Block" Prayer Walks

Hope Church started small: a handful of members walking the same three streets each Wednesday evening, praying quietly for homes, and leaving encouragement cards. Within six months, residents began joining. A local shopkeeper said, "I don't come to church, but I know the church comes to me."

Reflection Prompt: What would it look like for your church to be known for showing up—physically, prayerfully, joyfully—in your community?

✎ _____

_____

_____

_____

_____

CREATIVE ENGAGEMENT

Legacy Mapping

- Draw a tree. In the roots, write your theological anchors. In the trunk, your practices. In the branches, the fruits you hope future generations will see.

Movement Timeline

- Sketch a one-year plan for your ministry: three small initiatives, one celebration, one public witness.

Embodied Prayer Practice

- Read Gal 6:9 aloud while slowly stepping forward, pausing at "do not give up."
- Journal: How did moving with the verse deepen its meaning?

✎ _____

_____

_____

_____

_____

_____

_____

_____

Community Vision Wall

Imagine your foyer filled with photos of members in motion—walking, dancing, stretching, serving. What words would you paint across the top?

✎ _____

_____

_____

CLOSING REFLECTION

Sustaining a movement requires faith, patience, and vision. It is not about keeping busy but about keeping faithful. Leaders multiply, stories inspire, rhythms embed, and the church begins to move with its own steady heartbeat.

And when that heartbeat carries into the streets, parks, homes, and digital spaces of the world, the gospel becomes visible, tangible, and embodied. Sustaining movement is sustaining mission.

Guided Prayer

- Lord, thank You for reminding me that movements are built on faithfulness, not flashes . . .

_____

_____

_____

- Help me to raise up others who will carry this vision forward by . . .

_____

_____

_____

- May our legacy be one of faith in motion—until every body finds healing, rest, and joy in You.

Bibliography

Eime, Rochelle M., et al. "A Systematic Review of the Psychological and Social Benefits of Participation in Sport for Children and Adolescents." *International Journal of Behavioral Nutrition and Physical Activity* 10 (2013). https://ijbnpa.biomedcentral.com/articles/10.1186/1479-5868-10-98.

Ottey, Hezron. *Faith in Motion: How Religion Inspires Physical Activity.* Eugene, OR: Resource, 2025.

Van der Kolk, Bessel A. *The Body Keeps the Score: Brain, Mind, and Body in the Healing of Trauma.* New York: Penguin, 2014.

World Health Organization. "Physical Activity." June 26, 2024. https://www.who.int/news-room/fact-sheets/detail/physical-activity.

www.ingramcontent.com/pod-product-compliance
Lightning Source LLC
Chambersburg PA
CBHW052203090426
42741CB00010B/2388